BODY BACH

BODY BACH

MARJORIE BECKER

TEBOT BACH
HUNTINGTON BEACH • CALIFORNIA

Design, layout, cover design: Rolling Rhino Communications,
Melanie Matheson
Cover art: "Carmine Café", by Bill Brauer
Printed by: Westcan Printing Group, Winnipeg, Canada

ISBN: 1-893670-18-x
Library of Congress Control Number: 2005926359

A Tebot Bach book

Tebot Bach, Welsh for *little teapot*, is A Nonprofit Public Benefit Corporation which sponsors workshops, forums, lectures, and publications. Tebot Bach books are distributed by Small Press Distribution, Armadillo, Ingram, and Bernhard De Boer.

www.tebotbach.org

ACKNOWLEDGEMENTS

Other works by Marjorie Becker (selected):
"His Jesus Feet," in Paul Suntup, ed., *So Luminous the Wildflowers: An Anthology of California Poets* (Tebot Bach, 2003.)
"Why I Sleep Mexican Afternoons," *51%*, 1999
"Am I Only To See Lost Lovers?" *Haywire* (Haywire Press, 1998.)
"Bones," *The Cape Rock*, (Southeast Missouri State University, 1985.)
"Zubarán Lemons, Oranges," forthcoming in *RUNES: A Review of Poetry*
Setting the Virgin on Fire: Lázaro Cárdenas, Michoacán Peasants and the Redemption of the Mexican Revolution, (Berkeley: The University of California Press, 1996.)
"Talking Back to Frida: Houses of Emotional Mestizaje," History and Theory, (Dec., 2002.)
"When I was a child, I danced as a child, but now that I am old, I think about salvation: Concepción González and a past that would not stay put," in *Alun Munslow and Robert Rosenstone, Experiments in Rethinking History*, (New York: Routledge, 2004.)

To the memory of my mother,
Carrie Popper Becker

contents

IV. BLIND

V. PARENTHESIS

VI. THE VOICE OF DREAM: A POSTSCRIPT

forward

While I seem to write from obsessions as elemental as needs to experience color, music, rhythm, joy, to give life to the people who populate my imagination, perhaps my most profound longing is a wish to encounter like-minded people. Thus it is a deep pleasure to acknowledge the remarkable friends, relatives, and teachers, whose kindness and generosity summoned me to enter this world. I am very grateful to my friends in the poetry groups and classes in which I have been lucky enough to participate: groups meeting at Beyond Baroque, Midnight Special, the Church at Ocean Park, and most especially, what David St. John has called the "Monday Night Poetry Posse." In particular, I have been blessed by the generosity, talent, and many kindnesses of Jeanette Clough, Brendan Constantine, Dina Hardy, Beverly LaFontaine, Paul Lieber, Sarah Maclay, Holaday Mason, Jim Natal, Amy Schroeder, Brenda Yates, and Jan Wesley. I am more grateful to each of them than they will ever know. I am also deeply grateful to many other friends and teachers who (somehow,) saw something in me when I didn't: Alice B. Davis, Nita Donovan, Larry Goodwyn, Carolyn Gurman, Eva Maria Kadiev, Paul Lerner, Maria Elena Martinez, Roy Pattishall, Jim Ysidro. I have never been able to express enough gratitude to my beloved colleague and friend Gordon Berger for his friendship and kindness. It should go without saying that I am eternally grateful to my beautiful, brilliant and (thank God, funny!) sister, Joan Becker.

Because I served in the Peace Corps in rural South America, because by profession, I am a Yale-trained historian of Latin America, and because I am a professor of Latin American history and culture at the University of Southern California, I have had the great good fortune of living and working both in South America and Mexico. Without the aid of a number of national and international granting agencies I simply would not have been able to live in the places about which I have written so copiously (and with so much license!), many of which have been transformed into contexts for these poems. I am most grateful to have received fellowships and grants from the Fulbright-Hays Faulty Research Abroad Program, the National Endowment for the Humanities, The American Council of Learned Societies, the Ahmanson Foundation, Yale

University, the Hewitt Foundation, USC's Faculty Research and Innovation Fund, and most especially, USC's College Faculty Development program.

Perhaps because I have been fortunate enough to write, in various genres and forms for much of my life, I have come to know and cherish particular people who have proved adept at entering fabricated interior and exterior worlds, and at hearing (as I do,) the sometimes nearly inaudible, sometimes clamorous chorus of voices. I am thinking of course of Mifanwy Kaiser, who with grace and courage has proved willing to take on an almost completely unknown poet. I am thinking of my late Macon News friend, comrade, and city editor, Bill Maynard. I am thinking of my Yale graduate mentor Florencia Mallon who in a moment of great intensity and kindness, suggested I re-enter a subconscious world of creativity, beauty, and possibility. I am thinking of the remarkable historian, novelist, and editor Robert Rosenstone. And I am especially thinking of my colleague, friend, and poetry teacher, David St. John. Characterized by an intense *gracia*, an almost ineffable way of being, David quite simply believed in this work when I faltered. Without his genius and generosity as teacher and friend, it is hard to think this book would have come to be.

My mother, Carrie Popper Becker, died before I completed this book. She was a Vassar-trained mathematician, a woman deeply moved by beauty, a person of abiding passion and courage. As she frequently pointed out, she was a fourth-generation Macon, Georgia Jew. While she grew up in a world deeply compromised by murderous racial and religious hatreds, she herself felt nothing but reverence, respect and friendship for black people. While she grew up in a world in which poor people were frequently forced to go to bed hungry, she felt nothing but compassion, sorrow, and determination to do what she could to help. Her lifelong work for and with blind people was path-breaking. Notwithstanding her ability to accomplish anything she tried, notwithstanding her intense loyalty to friends and family, notwithstanding her dry humor, her genius for story-telling, and notwithstanding the fact that (as my beloved father correctly put it,) had any of us been stricken by the cancer that took her life, she would have single-handedly affected a cure, she possessed a singular modesty. On a clear and blue November day, throngs of people attended her funeral. Nobody would have been more surprised than she. This book is dedicated to her presence and to her memory.

—*Marjorie Becker*

introduction

A TAPESTRY OF THE SPIRIT

The Poetry of Marjorie Becker

Marjorie Becker's new collection of poems, *Body Bach,* is a startling and original journey of passage that recuperates the passions of a personal past—that past and its narratives are often woven into and against the lush backdrops of Latin American settings—while examining the conditions and dilemmas of the speaker's ever-defining and ever-changing present.

This is an adult's book, a hard-won and deeply original collection. Stylistically, Marjorie Becker has developed a truly fabulous way of simultaneously weaving and unraveling narratives so that time braids with and upon itself, and her meditations on the past become also, therefore, meditations on the present. Marjorie Becker's poetic lines are like strings of silver web thrown out into the world until a full tapestry is spun that is so delicate and so dense that we are able to see within its shimmerings, its mirror, our reflections alongside those multiple images of the speaker herself.

Yet the self posited by the speaker in *Body Bach* is as much reformative as it is reflective, as she constructs and reconstructs a way of negotiating the glorious impositions of the body upon the supposed verities of the spirit. The sexuality in *Body Bach* is raw and, at times, unmediated, as a way of calling our attention to the same shock of sexuality that confronted us as young adults passing into and through the strangeness—even into a loving strangeness—of the larger world.

It would be hard to overstate how much I admire the candor and beauty of these poems, as they begin like memoirs, then turn into dreams, and at last exist in our imaginations as nothing less than revelations, nothing less than recognitions of the lives we have all led. Fugal in its individual movements, rich and extravagant in its tonalities, *Body Bach* reminds us of the driving pulse of what D.H. Lawrence called "blood knowledge,"—and of all the lessons we desired and of all the teachers we sought out in the service of that singular and spectacular "body" of knowledge. As you will soon discover, the chords of *Body Bach* resonate long after the book itself has been closed.

—*David St. John*

SCAVENGER

LOOKING FOR AN OPENING

Maybe in Mexico he dealt
opals. Opals of the night and its conceit,
eraser opals rubbing out marriage vows,
those opals streaked with orange, red
no oceanic blue, no escalator sense of beach.
Just possibilities, a gift of opals
an entrée to the Zamable dance
at Clara's where his maybes would be
as firm as opals and anyway
it was Clara in mourning at her 50th.
I had loitered at home with Susana,
my Lebanese landlady,
not really wanted to be first
or even there at all
but feeling—for all Clara's Volkswagen
rides, attempts at picking up friends—
nobody much would be at the party,
feeling—and not for the last time—
that though clothes don't really matter,
makeup and jewelry less,
that I was badly dressed,
and full of surplus anxiety,
when lo! I stumbled in and her boyfriend
pulled me onto the dance floor,
fed me nopales,
an entirely new secret diet.
The opal man may have entered
behind me and as he danced
hard, he bent down, crouched,
tickled Clara's perfect feet
in her satin ballet slippers.
For the truth was,
Volkswagen or no,
she had enduring feet,
no bunions, no need to stumble,
and her hot Argentine smile
made its mournful entrance,
and the jeweler said,
even if her boyfriend was necking with the gringa,
you've gotta think of it this way,
he was only necking, and sure, plaintive enough,

but gringas always leave, and anyway
the gringa didn't drive or draw or paint as well as she,
didn't know Cervantes, that olive world,
Machado's silver olive tree world . . .
but really, if someone mentioned La Mancha's rival silvers,
he, his jewelry name Juancito,
wanted to leave, take the gringa back to Spain
where they met before,
and in actual fact,
this party could go to hell,
and take with it
the chingada, the fucked one.
But like all hungry wanderers,
he began to walk and walk.
Everybody knows the South is bad,
crap and beggar infested, crap and chicle infested,
crap and gringo-born chicle infested,
that men who could really dance
and only men who could really dance
hazarded the South.
He could dance and dance,
he could have stopped the gringa's
odd way, thinking English, dreaming English,
in Zamable talking only and forever Spanish,
he could have but instead
when his opals went begging,
the gringa's meaning too confusing,
when, the exact night he dreamed
of hard northern gin, a drink capable of holding ice,
when, and maybe when . . . but you know,
none of that happened because I myself was at Clara's
dancing drunk and guilty with her boyfriend just my age,
while the opal man walked, swam, squandered
a partial empires of maybes, in a low moment.

JUST STAY

Before I met you, Juan,
my girlfriends anointed me,
fed me figs and dates,
protected,
so look back at us then, I mean
now, me drenched in random
kisses and opals, any flesh.
There is the intoxication of light,
of deep inner humor,
hell with that,
when you touched me,
when you knew,
that Madrid siesta,
knew in the Biblical sense
and though I never stopped longing,
it seemed when I left Madrid,
forgettable. Just another guy
who maybe wanted my mane
of hair, my saddened eyes,
but something,
something . . .

We were four,
the program director,
Cuban and darkly brazen,
confused that she, Letitia Soborno,
eloquent and willful with Cervantes,
Lope de Vega, Becquer's beginnings,
Sor Juana, don't even mention Caribbean
in the same phrase with Letitia,
such a swimmer, so given to tides,
dulce de guayaba embraces,
the pain of flamenco gypsies,
art of life and darkness,
and this very afternoon,
here, here, in this restaurant,
in Spain's persistent fascism,
its hungers, its feasts of blood,
here, falling toward
the unspeakable,

toward a youngish woman,
Lila with her Peruvian bones,
as Quechua, Aymara,
as the living forgotten of Potosí,
its pools of naked silver and desperation.
Next at the table, Peggy,
the red-headed upstart,
her actual interest in others
unusual in extroverts,
and so spicy, luscious,
it should have been on the menu.

I was the small one with the green eyes,
young ways, enfolding a wildness dense
as the scent of tea olive, its secret destiny
not yet ready to flood, and they saw that,
protected me from men,
the verbal cartwheels of compliments,
street piropos,
linguistic trails I understood
and did not believe. My friends
rolled their eyes, clutched me
tightly. They called me La Maja,
knowing full well that I was not yet
the dark woman in hiding,
shawls encasing breasts,
her picture on department
store soaps, not yet . . .

My friends carried their personalities
as lightly as new makeup.
I usually couldn't,
but that day was my birthday.
We were in a Madrid restaurant,
on a back street, chords of Andalucía,
a time when people sang together,
gypsies teaching hymns, tunes.
The food when it came
perfect, but way verdura,
a world of vegetables
in the Spanish universe
so given to pork.

When the champiñones
in aceite, the alcachofas,
the perfect field mushrooms,
artichokes, tortilla española,
manchegan cheese arrived,
it was clear my friends
had ordered my favorites.

You came up, Juan,
with more wine.
You watched Letitia
nodding her head
as I threw back
mine, and you listened to me,
listened, like listening for ocean,
shell to ear, as my laughter
with its slow, nearly silent beginning . . .
but hell, I knew to laugh—
watch the chairs, the crystal,
the room—and as you certainly never forgot,
this was Franco's Spain,
but suddenly it seemed a dance floor,
or be precise
(your life dwelled in halls of precision,)
a whorehouse. You wanted that, me,
but watching me drink, knew
a shyness beneath the noise.
You somehow sensed I remained,
perhaps against my will,
pure.
Maybe you could fix that.
But for now, putting your hand
on Letitia's shoulder,
you listened. She asked for
dessert, a special postre,
said La Maja has just managed 20.
Could you bring something
special.

You said you don't know.
When I started this place,
I saw Madrid harnessed
forgotten energy,

ossified gestures,
open gazes gone stilted,
seized all that to make
ancient foods sparkle.
What could I do
in that market?
I shouldn't be here anyway,
my ancestors secretive,
but scattered, ragged
after 1492,
their persistent refusal
of pork.

I shouldn't be here,
but I captured a small birthday trade.
Que casualidad, Letitia said.
What a coincidence.
Hace falta something dense,
chocolate. A profound chocolate
need. You said wait,
plundered your kitchen,
brought me
a dark chocolate tart.
You kissed each cheek,
said to me in Ladino,
the Yiddish
of the Sephardim,
just stay a while,
just stay.

MEMORY OF A DANCER

I dance with old ladies, he said.
And steal their teeth?
No, he said, I went as thief
but they like to lose their rubies to me.
I planned to steal, I'd knocked
up a beauty, and the women heard
something about me. I sat alone
waiting. Dowagers, voluptuous old maids.
One by one, they found me. They are hot enough.
I know, I said. They are unassailed
emerald beauties. Whores.
Ándale. I kept all their gems
in a leather box, their names,
their colors on each. I have the memory
of a dancer, go regularly, return the jewels.
Again, again, they dance with me. They are hot
and return the gems, we kiss, the ring,
the bracelet on the tongue, in the cleavage.
If we dance tonight, when we dance,
it will be ultimate for them.
¿Porqué? Porque saben que he estado
esperándote, porque una mujer como tú.
¿Porqué? Why, you ask.
Because they know
I've been waiting.
A woman like you.
Are you mad with grief?
Only desire. Good, I'm right.
When we dance tonight, I'll feel
a lot about you, I dance with your own
instinct. Animalita. Animal,
and when I fuck you,
Ni decir. There's
nothing
to say.

SCAVENGER

I said why did you take so long.
He said I didn't expect you
to marry *stam* for cruelty.
You needed somebody older,
even at certain times a woman
longed, lunged,
but you're none of that.
Why a man so young, deep-eyed, mean?
I kissed without thought.
Random, misjudging,
I ripped his shirt,
remained the scavenger,
languages, water, places
by the railroad tracks.
He said I live by the eye of water.
Come over tonight.
I said no, you'll just leave.
He said only for jewelry,
Peruvian silver, coastal pearls.
It seemed precarious, too raw, too old,
but maybe I knew him before,
should have stayed in Madrid,
and this time, he lifted me,
my voice too awkward
to speak, though I believed
I met him first with Clara,
her head full of Argentine struggle,
so religious in her opinions,
her seizure of that smallish
Mexican town, worry about her age,
her boyfriend Pancho dancing me hard,
our bodies somehow fit
and Juan came in late,
kissed Clara. I saw,
out of the corner of my eye,
my man bringing Malaga itself,
the Portuguese coast,
Mediterranean figs,
kissing Clara.
I grabbed Pancho, clung.
Perhaps, though, destiny

keeps trying. Especially,
I think, for other people,
and Clara's Pancho tried to lift me,
said guest bed, said down blankets,
mentioned swan sheets,
but it was Clara's birthday
her possibilities lingered
and I was mad and drunk,
staggering toward the door.
Juan followed, said what, said why,
said don't worry, it's not quite our time,
come look, I have an opal for you,
dark, flecked with green,
the green of your eyes, don't worry,
I came a long way for this.
Clara, I said, but he took my hand,
said you have beautiful hands,
active, too, I know that.

It's true I wanted the Spanish Jew,
the man who knew how to dance,
fed me squid in Spain,
placed Mediterranean flowers
near my breasts, in my hair,
sang, gave me stray topaz, amethyst,
said his life was his restaurant,
said he missed Jews,
said please,
but virginal, I left him,
hot, aching.

Didn't you marry, I asked.
Again, again, but he picked me up,
had a strength somehow I didn't expect.
He was no fool, picked me up.
We danced, keen as railroad pitch,
the night train, its lonely wail,
a jelly jar, its silver top,
he was unscrewing a jelly jar,
licking out the preserve,
the ancestral fruits, peaches,
muscadine, licking me close
to the heart I once had, young,

swimming naked in green and blue
waters, pale light,
preposterous.

WHEN MARZIPAN HOVERS, WHEN NOUGAT

A world lingers near minor keys
when I lie. Think A minor.
Think what Bach, even Handel do,
their glories with major keys.
But think minor again:
the long, slow, tense,
painful build-ups.
The crooked, courtly wail.
The hope against buried hope:
Tense.
Wait, and in waiting forget
why you wait.
The final major key clamor, release,
your own stagger,
a dense moan of rain.

When I lie the minor persists,
repeats like collards,
and I was lying
about my divorce.
That I had one.
Had the sense Mexicans preferred
single academic women walking alone—
wandering the countryside for documents,
roaming for history,
seeking tattoos,
the being and litter of revolution—
to be married.
Wore my slender ring
the everlasting love words engraved inside,
lied.

Daily I went for a paper
walked into "Noticias,"
a hut of a store.
Followed the owner's sudden smile,
his eyes more familiar than God,
that deep brown Jewish guidance.
Without speaking we knew
we shared centuries. Our connection instant.
Not the usual struggle to somehow fit,

not offend. Wrong colors, styles, cadences,
wrong that oh yes, I know how to pick mushrooms,
so do all my relatives. Wrong that in that impoverished
world I swam daily in the early waters of the hotel
pool. Truly wrong: we are all one and here most
couldn't swim, couldn't read. Wrong and wrong,
but this man, this Benjamin,
there was no melodic struggle.
Instead a world paved with one minute,
rock 'n' roll, the next a dense mist of gardenia.

He somehow sensed my troubles,
said I'm sorry for what *he* did.
Turned and opened a worn—out drawer,
found me a necklace, and said my name.
It was amethyst. The bruise color
calmed by turquoise,
the bruise calmed
by patience's only color.
He said, let's swim tonight,
said I live by the eye of water,
said tell me what you're hearing.
I'd said nothing at all about Bach,
less about the minor key world.
He opened a box of Toledo nougat,
opened marzipan in golden foil,
fed me as though he had to,
fed me as the music changed
keys.

PLAYING SCALES

BODY BACH

Know this now as we begin.
I am yours as I couldn't be.
Your tricks of light, air,
those wild waters.
Leave you? Would again, but girl,
for this kind of life, this somehow fit . . .

I couldn't listen well,
stumbled on though his voice was emerald,
his voice was deep. Jews have seen, done
everything, as we talked, I jumped ahead
to the island alone, no voice, no man knowing
not just that I fucked around, but that I kept
him from his deepest propagation.
He couldn't start babies,
sperm didn't work right,
but had he been able,
I would have stopped it,
hard, cold, on the ground,
underground, he suspected,
fucked me partly out of spite,
but mainly, it was our body Bach,
a long ability to withstand that seeming infinity
of minor keys, my breasts tight, harder,
a work up, a forest of pain, no foreplay,
its reverse. We both knew that prelude,
we wrote it together in the sweet cottage
of a former life, before I recognized
part of every prelude had to be thick, deep,
gulps of a certain liquid, it had to be, before I knew
the taste becomes me, no, we were content then
to come together, something about our plastic limbs
our views of loyalty, permitted such a cottage,
full of river ferns, irises, he pressed iris whore petals
against my breasts, ate strawberries low,
frothy, but we didn't yet know
the role, our roles, we hadn't been shaken
away, and of course I went first,
this return would be based
on sorrow, buried sorrow,
sorrow that could not be answered.

The promise was, every time,
we worked together in ways most can't,
don't. Worked because of a long darkness,
he hit me some, his taste for blood,
we timed our cruelties, he told me
of recent women, he ate himself off me,
his heart remained tender, pained,
I was insatiable for ferns,
knew, too, when we fucked in a thick
bed of ferns, he would leave me
that night, though, was our return,
and we listened—a long riverless Bach,
and as we found each other,
I turned away.

JUST SOFT ENOUGH, HARD

That cold spring morning
the sun still uneasy with daffodils,
forsythia, with my tendencies
to stay away from you,
you pushed in.
It was nine
and the apartment air parceled itself.
The torn curtain opened to recent ruckus.
The night before
a stranger broke a window,
approached me with a shard of glass,
I fled next door,
ran barefoot to the black singing church.
The ladies looked up from their lush notes,
the chords so wet with feeling even I,
slipshod but Jewish,
could see the naked God.

I spent the night on a pew.

Before you dropped by,
I went home from the church.
The carpet of glass, linen curtains ripped,
air dense with alcohol.
You walked in.
I expected you to say,
come on girl,
I've got a broom.
You didn't,
just took me by the hand,
walked me to your place down the alley,
picked me up.
You took me to a mattress just soft enough,
just hard enough,
said do you want lemonade,
do you want a little gin.
Or do you want,
well, just tell me honey.
Too shy, I thought.
I said I want a lot.
Let's just lie down a while,
we'll figure it out.

SELL YO PIANO

Peter walked me one afternoon,
early Georgia spring,
past the empty white buildings
across the river, across the snoring
tracks, the 3 a.m. train waiting.
He knew an abandoned building,
he knew a black world I would
learn, later, when Angelo found
my limbs adrift, but Peter had something.
He had seen me practice scales,
my body slack, hands
without affection. He spent
an hour, hot, my drowsy hands,
kissing my neck, looking for change,
saw, thought: some sort of steel,
some sort of capture, what they did
to make me play away instinct.
He turned my face toward him,
it all seemed unlikely.
A blue-eyed boy.
Not the wanderer
I thought I needed.
The next door boy.
Observant. After Malcolm raped me,
Peter had brought skin cream,
had picked mountain mushrooms,
made me soup. This all seemed unlikely,
but there, there, he said, as I kissed,
ravenous. Still playing the repetitious
scales. There, there, he said, his hands
alert enough, cruel enough and gentle,
working under my blouse, there, there.
You were born to dance, he said.
Clank. Thud. I might have never
touched those keys again, never.
Sell your piano, he said.
You've got that dancer's body, but no,
I hadn't known the nature of obedience
until then, my legs suddenly aware,
alert, needy, suddenly knowing,
all of a sudden knowing

what ivory keys do, give,
suddenly as he groped deeper,
the world was wet hell,
springs and rivers I hadn't known.
I played like I knew how,
odd notes and sweet, melodies
from camp, from the camps, too
Elsa sang me after rescue.
I played, played, and as suddenly,
stopped.

SIDE-STEPS THE G-MINOR, A-FLAT WAIL

Me in Macon the second time.
Be straight. Yeah, me Jewish,
you Elijah for all I know.
Me born Macon.
You stranger breaking in,
me known for the shakes,
anxieties, weird courage.
You wanta be here,
this downtown apartment,
crap decorations?
Be my guest.
Me?
Gone to the next door black singing church,
the ladies in shiny polyesters,
tulles, hats, their voices capture time,
fill that wooden church
with world.
I stumble in,
barefoot, shaken,
they never miss a note
but one of them
finds me a shawl, a blanket,
a pillow, another sidesteps
the G-minor, A-flat wail,
runs to kitchen, brings me
corn bread, butter,
Coca-cola.

HOISTED THE RAFT

I became green, emeralds,
I adorn beautiful bodies,
the glass-glint, the glint of those fields,
meadows, soft enough, hard enough,
an eagle sunlight bestowing
springtime heat. Your body Wayne, oh
Wayne, I didn't know,
I was more innocent than you
knew, but you lifted me up in the green,
you built a raft, hoisted the raft,
me, breasts, legs, emeralds tight on my neck,
all of that ballast down to the ferry, arranged
me, us, on the raft, on the ferry,
pushed a little, then hard, harder.

RIPE MUSIC

Why are the ragged and lush souls
only in Latin America, only on infernal beaches,
cold, cold Peruvian beach waters, nuestra América,
and I am middle aged and hotter even
than Macon, my Macon alley days,
and you, Peter, oh God, that ripe
summer. I was desperate. Girlfriends give us shells,
silk scarves, see-through slides, small quartz prayers,
they listen as they move their fingers, crochet
or knit, one girl's name was Pearl,
I adore and adored all my friends,
my girlfriends some kind of stand-ins
for what had seemed too
hard, craggy. Long Vermont, Maine,
northern beaches, barren lands without touch,
my girlfriends tended to tease my Caribbean soul
but Leslie, her hot laughter, her promise,
I really don't want to know that's over now,
was gone and suddenly, Peter,
as I tramped around in that alley,
knowing I was never shy or frozen
around black guys, although I now know
this was not reasonable (or thought out) at all,
I say still, all
is flesh, there is only flesh,
when you wandered up to me, reached
out, long thin arms, eyes working me over
tumbling, singing, like song—see, song makes,
uses chords as creatures, creatures that—
and hear this, Peter—creatures that must
scuffle, wrestle, handle, pull
and of course fuck, and your eyes were chords,
and though we hardly knew our destiny—
it's easier to know it now after what
I am trying to say—you reached out, seized
my thin fingers, grasped, and I moved in
face to face. I knew you, and before
my mound of questions, a true and buried
Indian mound—maybe I shouldn't, maybe you wouldn't,
I'm going to have to go weak or desolate,
find a pose in a grocery sack or potato bin,

before that tedious riff,
I moved closer, quiet, closer, quietly
wandered into your music, let you seek,
let you find me. ·

RETURN

GREEN

Do I believe in any other green?
Sure. The field where I unzipped
Wayne, took him
whole, in many places, on top of,
surrounded by hard floors of green
hope. I wear only emeralds when I dance
at the Zamable. I no longer wait for Wayne,
for Arnulfo, for Daniel. No. After the Clara party,
Juancito made it clear. As long as I rose,
naked, to "Uno no puede olvidarte,"
or other next-door-to-the-Mexican-hotel ballroom jingles,
as long I remembered
the emerald rings, necklaces, spaced them
in a strategic way. Strategic, I thought,
I dance naked in emeralds, where else
will we go? But he knew at that point
he would return, return, like the song,
and at that point, Mama gone,
at that point, my limbs somehow
able as they never were,
I said nothing,
just rose, found the green serpentine,
jade, the tourmaline, the precious emerald,
roped my breasts, waist, pussy,
opened to the dance hall,
the dance hall.

RAW SILK

What does split consciousness do.
Were we to imagine, say, your purity—
your single consciousness.
Do it, check it out.
I am carrying your baby
and you never even said darling
only that my breasts were beautiful.
I work in a cloth store selling bolts of sun,
the yellow satins,
the violet silk
of wind
to women who have all the diamonds,
crystal, pearls I never will
and I listen,
listen.
They tell me who cheats—
Kenny, for instance,
and I know that,
he even brings me daisies,
cut saffron,
eats at my place,
and you say my brain is divided
and I say well, yeah,
so I quit the cloth,
walk to the dress store
(no more Woolworth's,)
and again, it depended on what I could eat,
would eat, suck, draw,
how well I pleased
the fancy ladies in the back,
from time to time the front, their men,
and they raved because I became
a half-time buyer for Mr. Frank,
the rest of the time,
again, why the surprise,
food, eating.

And you ask—not that you did, but had you—
what would be my feast
and I say it's not that I don't like you, I do,

but my own feast
needs to be near a naked stream,
a flow of green, a flow of blue,
there are small dewberries, strawberries.
Blackberries, he picks, de-thorns,
he finds places, they are secret,
they are hidden,
they are raw silk,
I learn, he had and somehow teaches
the ways of the Caribbean,
cruel enough to attract my attention,
he feeds and feeds,
brings me knives and chocolate.

The knives?

Just to remind me what was there,
what I came from,
the long descent
down stairs,
begging, yes, it's true
I did what I did for food,
the rules were I would be scared
so as not to be scared
and be sure to smile,
be pretty to gorgeous,
pretty to gorgeous,
here by this stream
we use the knives
to cut asparagus.

He cuts wood, builds fires,
I sing, wondering if he will
be able to, he comes toward me,
to plough, the tongue, the song,
the build of Bach, the stew,
the menestra of chords,
minor, the breath of minor,
the insistence on pain.
Get this: music never leaves
but before it doesn't, it pierces—
think what they do, did to ears,
the hot pierce and all those

clank chords and dirty—
who would have thought a Lutheran?—
wind around, a spill,
a spool spilling but also binding,
a lavender paralysis,
a lemon threat,
a wave,
and finally, finally
the tongue of release,
the mouth,
the weather,
the wind,
the groan.

BEGGING FOR CLARA

I love a sort of Mex-macho
that wants me and knows, after very little,
pretty words about my ways, green eyes,
heritage and carries a little money—
they feel they need to feed me more
than our late night supper.
They know it won't be Spanish olives,
purple grapes, browning dates of wonder
and ease, they know, too, it might be like
dancing hard at Clara's. Her boyfriend
hot and young, hot, younger,
agile, lifting me, limbs, Calmenson legs and all
(Everybody says us Calmenson women,
all arms and legs)
onto the hard dance floor.
His cascade of touch, clutch,
hours of color, Rivera feasts,
purple, red, rains of bourg. money
and late that night, my yelps
punctuating the silence. So much
for Clara, he said. Oh no, I said.
She will wake, lose weight, find her urge
for you, the urge I said, as I crawled
content enough, into his world.
For now, just sing to me,
I begged.

THICK STEW OF NOTES

He loved Arab men for chess play,
but his love of women, their flesh
without bounds. He kept his restaurant,
fucked and fucked, always leaving,
never violent with anyone, he walked
the streets of Madrid for early-morning
ingredients. Chose siesta women.
His eyes, such beauties women either
went still or followed him.
His memory extreme,
but that afternoon
the American Jew, her eyes.
So like his, her flesh,
he feared, untried.

A strange order.
Champiñones in olive oil,
tortilla española, but she also wanted
figs and dates, figs, dates and olives.
Biblical ware. Their eyes locked
as he scribbled her order, their eyes,
and he leaned toward her, hazarded
Hebrew, spoke broken English. So quietly
only she heard it. The message superfluous.
He arranged the fruits in a silver
filigree basket, a note.
Margarita, por la tarde. Quédate.
Stay this afternoon, Margo.
I want you to listen to me.
Anyway, I play a menestra
of instruments, a stew of notes,
hopeful and tough,
not what you want,
not even what you
think you need.
I'll bring your friends chocolate
laced with sleep drugs.
I'll show them siesta rooms,
the fat woman who wants me,
the other who adores you,

the one who protects,
but you chica, wait,
just wait . . .

ITS POWER, ITS SINGULAR POWER

I lived a lie there,
wore my wedding ring,
its slender gold binding me
to haphazard lies. The half-Persian
I had married after I taught him touch,
a world of grasp. My library carrel,
his. (His feet looking for mine.) Footsie in seminars,
once I'd loosened his fears, we found other places.
I tested floors for strength, durability,
possibility. At first, he found niches in alleys.
But you know, he got religion,
a religious voice said something like
she dresses too hot, loves too hard,
her past, all those people, men who liked to dance,
how do you think she became a dancer . . . ?

I was living a tiny lie,
they knew me married, if a little odd.
Why is she here, what work demands,
keeps her from her Persian man,
his eyes must be Jesus eyes and deep,
what woman would be in this crap village
and for so long. I wore the ring, spoke flawless Spanish,
thought English and rancor. I knew this:
yes he hit me that time, yes, yes, he broke my necklace,
yes he threw an ex-lover's pottery against
the wall, yes he told me how to dress, talk, act,
eat, pray, yes, I taught him how to fuck,
I taught him dance, its power, its singular power.
It seized his breath, I did, but nothing, even
our bedroom brawls, humbled him.

Juancito said we need another drink,
I said ándale, but it's Clara's night,
strangely, he said, oh no, pulled me tight.
I hadn't, wouldn't, couldn't believe he knew
the world he led me to, not just that he could
kiss, an art far more implausible than anything
else. I had known him while Clara painted,
took pregnant teenagers to clinics,
poured pitchers of sangría laced with promise,

did all and everything while her courtship scattered
and I went to the archive. At closing, I walked home,
and daily, sought out, found, a different passage.
Her boyfriend knew me, in the most casual sense.
He was the archivist. But once I worked late,
sweet-talked him into getting me, helping me
climb high, high into the stack.
I worked documents others failed
to see, to care about. This was a religious
place, hymns could still be heard at dawn,
though I lived in a hotel next to a sentimental dance
pavilion. At 3, ceaselessly, without fail,
"Uno no puede olvidarte," "One just simply can't forget you,"
began, dishes fell, clanked, I woke up, hoped the men hot,
deep-enough-eyed, the women lithe but busty,
hoped to God they knew how to dance,
promised myself I'd find out.

I met Pancho, yeah, Clara's Pancho
because one late Thursday
afternoon, I found a storage closet ladder,
climbed high, higher, up into the stacks,
seeking papers, seeking out truth,
or a certain facsimile.
Words. I hoped they would clarify
mysteries of betrayal, sodden pain,
but I missed a step,
I found the doc, yelped.
Pancho heard me as I clambered down,
missed one step, another, fell onto him.
You hurt? he said, but we were strangers,
as though we hadn't danced . . .
Clara, I said.
Fuck that shit, he said.
Clara's not here, we are.
Say you don't want. Tell me now.
He slowly worked on me. His move—
ok, all moves are dance, all moves
can be fugue. What I liked,
plainly required, was a person who could stop
the incessant rumble of thought,
broken fragments, rancid words,
who knew music well enough

to play, to play the sheer rose world
of play, lilacs, but also bed sheets.
We became a tangle of notes, legs,
sound, the night fell heavy there,
must, library must intensified my sullen need
for discordant notes yet this guy, just a guy,
just Clara's guy, didn't stop.
He said you are hungry and I was,
he said take off your bra
but we were beyond that.
I want you here every day,
he said, before the crowd or during,
I have my ways.

THE MAN WHO DANCED ME IN SPAIN

fed me squid,
oceans of sea life hand to mouth,
placed Mediterranean flowers
near my breasts, in my hair.
He sang, showed me a stray
topaz, an amethyst, said his life
was his restaurant, said he missed
Jews, said please, but I was a virgin,
left him hot, aching, virginal.
Didn't you marry, I asked
after the Clara party,
and he said, again, again,
but he picked me up,
he had a strength I somehow didn't expect,
my own bothers me, I hide it.
He was never fooled, picked me up,
we danced keen as railroad pitch,
the night train, its lonely wail,
the jelly jar, its silver top.
He unscrewed the jelly jar,
licked out the preserve,
the ancestral fruits, peaches,
muscadines, licking me even closer
to the heart I once had, young,
swimming naked in green and blue
waters, pale light,
preposterous.

ITS SPICES

The situation man holds me now,
walks me, clinging, to my kitchen,
taunts me: "We can fuck here."
But my own squadron of lovers watch,
wait, sing the tingle, sing the onion
of their hearts, the business about looking
back. I am here. I own the kitchen,
its spices, its wafers, its combinations,
berenjena, tomate, oregano and my own firm,
still valid limbs. Think about it.

I *own* the kitchen.

Little more, but hey,
do you want satin, silk?
Do you want my deeper flesh, my streams
and rivers? You know what I know,
know there have been hundreds before you,
and I know your thousands. And I know,
Juancito, the dance steps, yours with opals,
yours through fear that you will be mañana,
back in Cuenca, your fingertips still moist
from my deep hell places.
I own this kitchen. I work here, I cook here,
and every horny morning, Pablo brings me nuts,
berries, a new hoard of spices, game in season,
flowers for the table, the window ledge, my tits,
and brings me warm pleasures, warm release.
I own this kitchen, and Juancito, you know
what you know, you fuck and you fuck,
but I know the dance hall, I know contours,
I know underwater silk and grasses,
and baby,
I know how to yield.

NEED

We all know the quality of men,
especially before female sandpaper,
severe, sharp, quartzlike in limitation,
but women whose love is like a hot bath,
women easy to fall into,
without recrimination,
women like silk,
strong, soft, glamorous, moist . . .
There are only seven or eight left.
The others want yo money, want yo time,
yo jazz fuck, yo blues fuck,
yo attention, but not for yoself.
They try to make him, the big Him,
jealous. The 7 or 8 don't have time
for anything but you. For feast.
Your warm flesh bread.
Your hot bread flesh.
And you are big and bigger around her
and you know where to go,
moments like wave, like binding tape,
binders' twine, the 7 or 8 are not easy
to find. One or two live in alleys
three or four are certified whores,
so let's say six, or lucky seven,
lucky about her thighs,
has returned to Diego in Chile,
so there is really only one, hair long,
touching her ass, thighs, hands
suggesting what tonight will be,
the air thick with eyes, with mouth,
with hints, with breasts, you are suddenly
aware of the nature of shortage.
Odd. Before this wet encounter,
it is raining everywhere, all over,
before this, you felt glad enough
at home, glad to run unseen,
unheard, tamed into a world
without recognition, doomed to a few
missionary moves, it was all ok enough.
This is different. She is the last one,
water is everywhere, and you just know,

you moisten your lips,
you know in a cunning way,
you quit thinking, strip her slowly,
pick up her lithe body,
pin her down,
pin, wait.

ZUBARÁN LEMONS, ORANGES

The library was dark enough
and he was Puerto Rican and gorgeous,
his instincts, I mean, brain and more
than hope. He didn't think I'd respond,
he saw the slender
love-you-forever bind you, blood,
yeah, I hit-you-on-purpose-bitch ring,
saw that, but I surprised myself.
Eduardo. We groped in stacks,
he brought me membrillo, quince paste,
dulce de guayaba and Mex cheese,
he brought me his fingers, ate
himself off mine, ate himself,
ate the depths, the intensity,
and I told him mis palabras,
my words, my Spanish words,
came from Carmen, la bella bella.
She taught me there are certain words
and one night, an invitation to dance,
stark Puerto Rican flamenco,
a naked flamenco, she showed off,
I learned many tricks from her,
y palabras, yes, words, Eduardo, palabras.
Eduardo lived in an Orthodox Jewish Mexico City barrio,
lived among the very souls
who taught my bearded husband
it was ok to hit me out of rejection,
a sorrow he manufactured,
out of fear my ways he found exotic,
Egyptian, other Mediterranean alleys,
to pummel, at least to try,
the Talmud had nothing hard to say
women were unmentionable fucks,
parenthetical,
but the neighborhood people,
this was *México*,
had also fed me in my weakness.
My husband fled, anyway,
back to the Phoenix stables,
raising horses, he trained fillies himself
so I could avoid his hand,
and this neighborhood,

that assumed my long sleeves, skirts,
the ways I covered for him,
or had until now. That Sunday
Eduardo wanted to take me to a museum,
pictures inspire, he said, though of course
less than your skirt with its appliquéd shells,
your black hair, the silver glints,
your green eyes, your breasts,
the pictures, he repeated,
but said he was *resfriado* with the flu,
so please, please come over.
I took the metro, I took a bus
I had oranges in my bag,
oranges the size of breasts, lemons,
Zubarán oranges, lemons.
I worried, will the neighbors
spy for my husband,
feed me quietly,
thrill to a quick end
to that quicksand desert,
but I was dressing to please,
tight skirt, short, my own clothes,
I was wearing bright pink,
carrying Zubarán oranges, lemons.
When I got there, Eduardo was weak,
draped himself around me,
we were together on his purple
sofa, he traced my face, touched
everywhere, I will sicken, I said,
yes, he said, sicken with me.
I'll take you to bed,
and it was true,
I couldn't stop myself.
My body followed a logic,
but what? My husband might
hurt me like before
but here in this wishful space,
Eduardo began to eat lemons quietly,
bite ravenous oranges,
sicken me, sicken me,
lift me, feed me
and Eduardo, oh Eduardo,
somehow make me well.

FLOWER TINY ENOUGH

In all that time,
oceans of time,
Caribbean,
I never said,
less laid claim
to whom I really loved.

Open the silk:

the world of red and purple silk,
the tent room of my treasures,
small vases of iris, forsythia,
the room fragrant with tea olive,
a flower tiny enough, potent enough
to seize not just this minute—
arise, Enrique, Carlos, Juan—
but to attach itself
to past glamour, your blonde,
her thighs, the openings, possibilities,
the ways to seize and control cruelty.

I never said who, how, when.
Enrique, I'm saying now.
I acted like I didn't mean to.
I did, me in my long skirt,
appliquéd with shells, island shells and ocean,
but oh God, you found ways in, found me
waiting.
My marriage, a startling link,
not just the flows, though that rain
placed me into a world
of daytime soap opera, white trash fantasy.
You were my trash reality
and you found me in libraries, by rivers,
eating tacos with red beauty tomatoes,
in my apartment, yours, found me,
pulled me level and down
to your salty Caribbean,
your past lost in navels and touch,
jealousies and evening harvest.

AS GIRLFRIENDS GO

She was a suspended peach,
a quick molasses,
I would have bought her at the store,
traded my turquoise jewelry,
even amethyst, long gulps of light,
but she didn't know my marriage,
how he mortgaged what I taught—
not the ways of touch,
but the stuff itself, panting,
pushing through the window,
not the sound of fucking,
but touch itself. She didn't know
he hit me, stole my money,
broke my pearls,
took away my hidden words,
placed them in a frozen food locker.
My girlfriend didn't know. I would pay for her
still, but that night, see, my new man came by.
No, she said at the door. Who is this. I'll get rid.
I'll guard you all night.
You can't tell him, I said,
you don't know how.
I went to him, and he said lie.
I like to think I wouldn't, didn't,
but right then I said Armida,
he's leaving for Puerto Rico,
you go home, honey,
go on home.

OJO DE AGUA

He said we need this place,
this ojo de agua,
this eye of water.
Remember the time, hot, hazy,
your limbs worn like rust, when you couldn't
find the water's eye, and you were right, others pushed
you aside. Not a native. Just a woman.
Gringa, puta, whore, but the eye of water
didn't mind that, and honey, you know I waited
for the world, the water, your fluid,
happenstance heart, your tongue, to open
to its own wet possibilities, its naked
preferences, its habitat, my habitat
again.

BLIND

ABLE SILK ALIVE

What is turquoise?
Not seen on trees,
in spirits, in lightning.
It entered my life near Mama's
death. There was a back story.
A meditation on cruelty,
boyfriend turning against
my lush possibilities,
freezing them out.
The meditation itself a world of green,
a soft meadow by the chords of water,
me wearing platinum, gilded,
a host of people, friends, lovers,
they hugged me back.

I had told Mama only
the guy hurt me—I wanted
a little green birthday jewelry.
As the cancer hovered,
I sat by her, the time
so slender between us,
so slender, and she, blind,
felt her remaining hours·
in her still-fiery Vassar brain.

She said go to the dresser,
you'll find a white box.
Her jewelry, though, had been taken
to a vault, her fearful orders.
Still, I found a necklace,
broken up bits of turquoise.
The ways greens nestle blues.
I took it to her.
She felt.
That's it, she said. It's from Egypt.
Great Great Aunt Ess, maybe Rosaline
Greenberg brought it. Mama fingered again,
said do you want it,
and I didn't say yes,
I could never say what I wanted,
what I wanted then,

what I wanted
now, at this late
impossible,
my desire for nothing but soft
crooning, able silk alive.
And get this now—
this tenderness, mine,
but because of her,
scorned by her,
in her, in me.
I said instead
it's beautiful
and she said
happy birthday.

THE BLIND

What, though, if she is there,
still, in that hue of dirt,
Georgia dirt, not clay, she told me
before,
before the hospice
before she completely
gave up scrumptious little morsels,
Joan's squash casserole,
her husband's heat, him.
Oh God, another source of late pain,
water pain, those pains so unplumbed
on the German Jewish side,
before she quit eating daggers
and cheese straws, her own unique
treat, rather famous in Macon,
less so than her work for the blind

the blind

because see, the cancer was in her brain
and thus her beautiful legs fell, fell,
against a cold metal fan, seized
her one good eye and she quit
eating the scrumptious things,
the breathing hard, I sang to her,
full throated, bad voiced, my throat
choking with little girl sobs, and she told me
of making me the stuffed green zebra and fawn
"You couldn't buy them," and green
was my favorite, and the lake is deep,
I feel she is cold, feel hard and in pain
that I will give up my salary,
its years of multiplication,
the sapphire bracelet she gave me,
even my piano, any and all I have
to make a nice blanket,
maybe cashmere.

COVER

Felt Mama might be cold,
So sorry the student movers stole
my Sharon Elizabeth quilt, not rose of Sharon,
but my girlfriend Sharon, her lover Liz,
they made me a quilt of lavender scraps,
of purples, because I liked colors of glint
and regal possibilities, because they took me
to abortion—the boy in flight—because
Sharon rocked me, knowing she wasn't the guy I loved,
my eye's then apple, my private need for that darkness,
knowing I would be so cold with him, without him,
without, finally, at least, a quilt,
and now, so long after,
Mama buried with flowers though some idiots
decided Jews don't need, believe in flowers,
refused us, but I got Jimbo to put aside his recent exile,
send flores, and Ruthie brought house flowers,
the kind of lilies pretty for the day before
the scent corrodes, and on top of Mama in that hole,
Mama so thin but dressed in a favorite silk,
on top, dirt, Jews believe in dirt,
and yellow roses like the roses climbing
our balcony, the one Wayne seized me from,
took me to his plain floor,
hard enough and his body
perfect enough, tender enough,
silk enough.

PARENTHESIS

MY BRAIN A DANCE FLOOR OF ITS OWN

I.

The boy I danced with broke away.
Clara's boy. "I've gotta go," he said.
Ándale, I said, as alone as I had been
in his arms. The heat of dance,
his savage hands, a distraction
and very pure beneath the thin layer
of booze, but I didn't really want to take him
from Clara, her flint soul, near-German. In
consideration, I stood still. My brain a dance floor
of its own. A large space filled with
a blaze, a fire by a slender stream,
I dance naked best of all,
swim better, dive to the bottom,
examine river flowers, especially
purple ones, I was in that space,
when opal man came on to me.
He didn't mess around,
he'd come to mess around,
he whispered no more Clara,
no more Clara's place. You wanta walk.
Where, I said. Tengo despacho. An office.
Opals, I said.
Your eyes, he said,
opals of the night.
I'm drunk, I said.
He said nah, just a dance floor ruckus,
look back at Clara's,
listen for it. I did but there was no stray
rock 'n' roll, they were gone.
Come, he said. I was light and lithe,
the underwater swims, the return,
sour, intolerant.
My Spanish traced
the surface of this crap town,
its sorrows, stolen until summer rains,
when the valley turned emerald again.
I saw you alone walking, he said,
walking it off.
I live in a house

by the sometimes lake you traced.
Its contents in your feet, legs, hot begging,
its depth, you swim by night,
swim with me, I said.

II.

Not yet. He took my hand.
I talked to myself in English
for a while, but my hedge
had been broken. Not that Juancito
brought me ferns. My husband-that-was
picked the reds, pinks, oranges,
coded flowers to my then body parts,
coded by color,
and though he wanted religion,
and I wanted only heat,
I could still—
after all the rancid years,
feel his pressure, mine,
long for that first surrender.
Juancito knew what he was doing,
he didn't bring ferns,
or lavender iris.
What do you hear.
I said nothing.
I will name you.
Margo, he said,
but you have to know this,
slut that you are and trust me,
I feel that clamor, that vibration,
your silken need as I steal the wedding
diamonds. Women here. I do most of them.
Usually they pay me in gems, but I have
the most obvious access. Without fail
they reveal. An engagement sapphire,
a raw buy. Nobody suspects, I said.
Don't be simple. They know.
Their craving for deeper moves,
my single-minded ways, keeps them.
Tell me you didn't lie yourself, cheat.
You think in English
because your hidden body,

your dark-husband-clothes
are supposed to protect.
Come on.

III.

It wasn't like me. He gave me
no ferns. I couldn't stop myself.
My body no gift, but rare,
A deep rhythmic tune,
I walked toward him,
stripped without thought,
kissed hard. We finally found
our Sephardi grammar,
his tongue promising
that forgotten garden,
the wild figs, grapes,
black and broken and whole,
his tongue and that forgotten garden,
my tongue made relentless.
How much do you know,
I asked.

IV.

Whore, Juancito said.
He was thinking in Arabic,
in Ladino, in French,
He was thinking
about my Jewish needs,
"You're still looking, am I right? Don't lie."
He had pinned me down.
You explode the form, he said
and you just don't care
any more. Listen, he said.
No whimpering.
No later-on tears.
He opened a deeper drawer,
pulled out a velvet bag.
Taste these. He thrust
an emerald, a sapphire
in my various places.
Taste them.

Why do you think
I followed you to Clara's?
I saw you at the bus station
when you came. Your wild hair
ignited in the rain.
You came by rain.
I knew you before,
he said, pulling me closer.
Hágame el favor de escucharme
¿Porqué? Le dije.
Porque el ritmo adentro
es duro, duro, los gringos tan mecánicos,
cuentan, se tienen que besar
5 minutos, (así dicen sus manuales,)
y ni piensan del mundo que hay abajo,
el mundo mismo
mi menina,
tu mundo de colores, luces, acciones,
tu mundo más querido,
el mundo donde te invito
por el resto del tiempo, el resto.

Tattoos are hard to remove, I said.

You are not seeing this clearly.

Te tengo que decir que
dejaste el tipo, el tipo,
y su mundo de flores
baratas, cada rosa, iris,
escogida según un código,
algo rarísimo, claro,
pero todo legal.
Te estoy diciendo
una cosa. Que escuches,
con tus Carlitos, Sebastián.
Fuck you, Margo, it's me
Juancito. Te chingo y más,
cada día, noche,
vivo adentro, vivo al lado
de tus senos, tu alma.
Tu hot begging whore alma.
Te estoy diciendo.

Te esperé por mucho tiempo.
Al principio tu viejo, su mundo de flores,
después, sus manos llenas de pena,
tan dulce, tan dulce pensabas,
para ser brutal.

Lo que te hago es distincto. Ni me esfuerzo
por borrar la pena. Ni me esfuerzo.
You need something else.
It's simple, it's not
arithmetic,
foreign language, trapeze,
it's just me, Margo,
and we'll fuck in soft iris,
petals of roses, and you'll know
I'm screwing around,
and you'll endure
because you need the roses,
but more than that . . .
yet I quit hearing,
ni idea de lo que dijo
because we were outdoors,
close to a begging wall,
I decided to stay
not in the old dog-like way,
a sea of licks,
as though tongue work
generates a glue pulling together
shards of glass, pulling,
allowing old pain to scatter,
its liquid to flow,
not in the old dog way,
because he touched my hand
and though it felt unsayable, even in thought,
my mind chattered, spread,
a canasta without the pink plastic tray,   ·
a sentence with no verb,
my body knowing, clearer than sky,
sex, whoredom,
live,
awkward:
this depends on belief in water,
aqua and turquoise,

sheer belief, gossamer in structure,
nothing more, firmer,
only faint, nearly lost
handstand memories,
memories of true recognitions
that hankered to sustain,
nothing firmer,
I turned to him,
said softly, yet plainly,
teach me how you swim.
and he said, swallow,
placing a slender sliver
of manna in my mouth,
he pushed, his hands coarse,
alert (as only hands)
I swam deeper than I knew how,
the circle of silver water and green,
this was not particular, meant,
written, inscribed, but my limbs
found their native way, his,
I pulled out, shivering,
I pulled out, he dried me
outdoors, close to a begging wall,
a time piece,
close to each other,
a summer swimming naked,
a summer under the ojo,
the eye of water,
his dark Sephardi eyes,
his eyes, a possibility.

THE SUMMER WITH JUAN

I swam daily. The eye of water
had filled that torrential spring,
I swam into color,
the greens, blues of turquoise,
the turquoise the hot ladies gave him,
gems for flesh,
the greens, blues clinging together.
Swimming into one another,
as I swam into purple.
My bruises, jealousies,
always productive, alert, wandered off.
I swam, stripped, dressed
in tight clothes. I hoped Juan
knew why I stayed. I went inside,
woke him, a rain of kisses,
he played with me, told me
of his night ladies, then counted
one hundred rubies, plied me with red,
a seizure of blood memories, relations,
found the secret places,
watched me wrestling
in the dark and light.

THE WHORE I WANTED TO BE

I think why emeralds,
though that night, in the hotel,
the Felix, old riffraff boards,
these mountains are made of trees
so green, green, nearly sparkling against
blue, blue water, blue air,
my shivers, my skin quivers,
you lift me up. Find an old knife,
a knife paved with silver inserts,
cut off my clothes, lift me, tight
as a beggar, my wet hopes, I didn't expect
this. Thought I wouldn't see you after
Spain. Thought you wouldn't wade the currents,
wouldn't bring me, feed me, hot dates,
a basket of bleeding figs.
I need this and that worries.
It was an addiction I left—
that Spanish month, your wooden house
at the base of the Cuenca rise,
nestled between rivers, the old, outlined
in brown leaves, the young, a trail
of topaz. You carried me away from the usual
kiss kiss, touch me up. I wanted,
still want to be a whore.
A romance in my brain.
The beauty of the salon, the lace, the fire,
the kindnesses, a willingness to bend
toward need. I wanted to be a whore
and after you placed a ruby between
my breasts, Colombian emeralds
in my socks, I didn't worry the money.
I didn't turn whorish
because you taught me
to fuck openly, to love
your generous flesh.
I left because your flesh
addicted me. You stole my will,
I quit painting the sounds of Bach,
crocheting mantillas. I lived naked
with you. Naked, the limbs clothing enough
themselves a complicated fabric store,

legs as tough as silk,
breasts billowing like cotton sheets,
yet the attention, especially to your body,
took time. I did nothing
but dance.

TOO GOOD

He left
the trunkful of words,
the floor curved, still worn,
the indentations, the maze of deeds,
the Cuenca, oh Cuenca,
up from the yellow-lined river
a promise, really, and parallel
to the brown leaves huddling close
clinging to the bank of the older river,
Cuenca of hanging houses,
perfect for the menestra,
the stew, the dense connection
of their touch. He left.
It was, he said, too good,
too silken, too fleshy,
and sweet.
It made him want to die.

SHE LEFT HIM

A failure of dance.
Her personal trick,
to never be quite satisfied,
always need somebody, somehow
to move slow enough, calm and gentle
and hot, to fix her personal failure,
a critical vein voluminous
with blood.

He fucked everywhere.

This was not her excuse.

And it wasn't his divided attention.
He brought gems for her limbs,
emeralds matching her sultry eyes.
Topaz complementing skin near her navel,
ankle amethysts, rubies.
He knew her stretch of sorrow,
that S. hit her because
he came to need,
(it entered his most liquid veins,)
to scare her,
that terrified, she let him.
Something about that edge,
the broken cotton scrap of neglect;
she was told to consider the moths,
surely hungrier than she.

Juancito knew that,
massaged the grief itself,
knew her quotient, ability,
need for friction,
wouldn't leave.

And even that
was not her reason.
She left him, came back too,
because he needed her.

He came home a lot, never lied

about the alien pleasures, even people she knew,
and better, with less gesture, effort.
He changed her in a particular way,
she needed exactly what she had,
the dance steps inexplicable,
a mystery beyond body, flesh, after,
beyond death, the molten gold of their
bodies, the ways of electricity,
the inexplicable questions answered,
she never thought, just found
the tug of his skin, the fence,
clothes were necessary, unnecessary,
what one feels, gets
through cotton.
She left because of the denseness,
hers, his,
his, hers,
he had to,
she had to,
she told herself
(it was a lie)
she wasn't the creature he thought,
the being.
She wasn't, but she was, too.
The language never came close
to what they did, the luxury their lives
there, waiting over,
there,
by the eye of water so full,
overflowing with ecstasy, chocolate,
laughter, grasp, them.

PARENTHESIS

I read somewhere of truth.
Stories beg, after all
for proper silken endings.
That truth,
that true truth touch, ¿verdad?
Isn't this right?
Ferries a person to unseen,
noiseless inner worlds,
not just anybody does it,
knows it,
but as I read,
my body—
well, take it from me—
I'm not being coy,
that was why I left, Juancito.
I was scared,
I couldn't touch the fear,
needed to be able to scale it,
piano fingers, practice,
to chord the fear,
was it exotic, erotic?
how could it fit?
And I was young,
I needed certain repetitions,
stalled dances, stables,
the truth is, Juan,
Eduardo and those Caribbean waters,
the ways we fought, oh God, the fights,
the brambles, bruises,
were somehow nearly familiar
enough salve.

Except for this.
I, he, Eduardo and me,
we were still outside.
But then you returned to find me,
and I remembered non-story, non-entrance,
paths strewn with thorns, rocks, sores,
but that Clara party night you lifted me,
stam, just like that,
as the Israeli Hebrew speakers say,

the Hebrew speakers
in Nice, Santiago,
Guatemala City that was.
You lifted me up,
we skipped the dance,
the riffraff boards,
wailing hotel,
sweetmeats and sour,
you lifted me,
took me screaming.
Abduction was way low on my list.
I'm too clingy for that.
Any old sort
of discomfort preferable.
Clash of colors, reds, Bolivian pinks,
clashes of souls.
Really? You asked.
Really.
And besides, your arms were
perfect. You were
strong enough,
as strong as I was lithe,
you rearranged my limbs,
carried me,
my legs (*beckoning*)
containing your flesh,
your legs (*containing*)
beckoning mine,
we had discovered parentheses.
Say this. Gold foil, itself luscious,
(those chocolate smears, crumbs,)
contains the good stuff.
The foil a parenthesis,
and our bodies, Juan,
well, I just hadn't
known.

FED ME

I wouldn't stay, I felt, I thought,
I was so used to fucking against darkness,
against songs. My beauty too weak.
Also intense. Witness
the tangle when a hapless boy
tries to help me into my jacket.
Look, in a bar a man will pick me up,
but not if there is any sort of chatty,
tawdry blonde, and I know it.
Like the hundreds before me,
I stayed with Juan.
It wasn't just that he made me eggs,
eggs on corn tortillas, field mushrooms,
cut then in olive oil, cut them, fed me
with his hands, fed me ravenous and naked.
It was one question:
how can this have been?
He got it. Ok. This is the end of the book.
This is what I cannot admit or do.
If I say this, I die.
Not just that he got my marital,
my *martial*
truce and surrenders,
Puerto Rican fuck on the side,
my excursions to the book store,
flesh looking for flesh,
the motorcycle rides,
I knew Juan fucked the soul ladies,
the jewelry girls, and I knew
it was more than casual
and I was a fool, too. I knew
the hell of my soul,
the way it clings,
its lake of remorse.
I am saying this:
Only Juan,
his flesh settles me,
stops the verbal cross currents,
histories and purple blows,
my willingness still

to be bought,
the ways my in-laws
promised antique cameo,
birthday Baroque,
a Bach trio waking me, their son,
to some new flight.
Juancito is jealous, never stupid.
Doesn't craptalk my living past,
just uses what we have.
The ways we met.

He doesn't say stuff
like he doesn't want Gina, it's just
when his flesh finds mine,
his flesh finds.
The silver ceiling fan turns,
he raises the windows, listening.
I lose my steel. Bend, break
into Russian shrieks, driveway howls.
I am crying to the eye of water,
I am crying for him,
I don't want him to leave,
don't want anything more,
no emerald, no chocolate taste
of rubies, down my throat, elsewhere,

I don't need his Bach chords,
his music, his body purpose enough,
a shelter for longing,
ripened peaches, old railroad ties,
a smell of new wood, the carpenters
I fuck, their smell, their sound,
I am not clean, purity makes no sense,
I somehow know
I don't have to think
this through.

THE VOICE OF DREAM: A POSTSCRIPT

THE VOICE OF DREAM

He went to Mexico.
His sister, night-gorgeous,
wanted, well, him,
And he did too but
he was too clingy for her,
sought flesh, all sorts,
to still his nerves, his need
to be felt. She was marrying
again, he'd send her black topaz,
night amethyst.
A gentle enough plan, he thought.
He didn't imagine Margo again.
Hadn't expected to scare.
His plush bed, soft, soft,
the hard floor.

Listen you. I'm real.
I fuck hard, needfully at dawn,
at purple night. Don't write me out
of your coded diary,
your dance book. You didn't think,
believed your archival glances,
the curious Caribbean, hands, hands,
danger. The floor of flesh,
thought that was ok enough,
didn't believe I knew
you'd somehow. Hell, I came
an errand for my sister,
wasn't sure how.
It's this Margo.
Flesh stories start, begin.
You were tough young in your looks,
your moves, a tease. Still, no,
still, I lavished, tried to, at least,
your world. You were scared in ways
I hadn't. Hot in ways I knew.
Remember the sibling rivers
at the base of Cuenca's hanging houses,
a river filled with wind-catch, yellow leaves,
Peggy's smile, you might admit that need
though now you act like you're somehow beyond . . . .

The other river with its darker stains and comforts,
and if Peggy touched you toward early hopes,
dreams, afternoons, gypsy picnics,
she liked to feed you, no, she didn't know enough,
you might want to mention that in words for a change,
do you somehow imagine I don't,
the other river black in its glorious rage,
I thought, think,
you need a world of instinct,
soft, quiet, precise, green gems,
your eyes, heedless lingerie, soft enough,
tight enough, no lingerie at all,
a man who can get you
in and out
of your jackets,
your clothes.
You also needed.
Fuck the boys
who miss this,
your husband, say.
Something old chained you.
You needed somebody, say me,
who knew how to hold you.
The entire icebox of flowers,
the rare ones, orchids and pinks,
winter anemones, flowers that open
expectant, the fields of your
childhood fucks, tongue, tongue,
somehow you were suspended,
the need for soft intelligence.
You want me to beat you
into submission? No? No?
I think, thought it then,
thought you left, a body fear,
a hunch you wouldn't get anything,
a hunch you knew,
an insight into the real.
Your husband cruel enough
to be familiar, but distracted.
He thought you slut
almost turned you into,
don't lie any more,
it won't help,

but the Caribbean guy,
I'm surprised you didn't stay.
The climate.
It seemed right, ¿verdad?
Isn't it true?
Your need,
broken up, moistened,
His hands, fragrant from you.
His body tough
As silk. He lacked
your old man's insecurities:
you were his first, no?
You taught him,
slow learner, refusing you,
making you slut around,
making you. I came back.
There are stories waiting,
There are stories open as
stories work this way—
limber as silk, tough,
crawling, sea lizards, a woman's body
anxious in a room, bored,
a tent of language,
an unquiet intellect,
her legs tapping
to an unsung tune,
night memories
and pale. She doesn't, you don't
quite remember the way I entered,
our nights over the restaurant,
I didn't stop prowling.
Just knew stories crave
the whole jazz of being,
turn out the lights, we fuck
by morning air, mornings are long here,
last to, last past siesta.
The first stars in your pussy,
mornings last, you read once,
of a couple whose limbs
led them beyond, past,
toward what was truly inner,
previously inert, deep,
you knew as you read,

believed the writer had hypnotized
had interviewed your hot tight,
your moist life,
you and your Caribbean.

If I get this, I get you,
so this is how it went, no?
You told your husband what you had to have,
He refused, brought black roses,
head scarves in dull lavender,
a store-bought sea shell,
you sighed your minor key sigh,
he fled, carting away your hope
for the underwater cloth store,
the return of those nights with him,
when he didn't realize he turned you over
to an inner place,
you under water,
trapped by a naked mouth,
a small boy in need,
your legs, easing through
an ooze trying to encase
the child suckling,
an explosion of milk descending,
multiplying like manna,
you swimming, the weight changes,
a sudden buoyance, thunder, you under water,
eyes wide,
you under water
and yes, swimming through sea aisles
of ribbon, of rope,
golden scissors, thimbles with initials,
an underwater cloth store,
gold and silver satins
but the rolls of silk,
turquoise, their pale aqua relatives,
blue scrambling in,
and the songs, the songs,
the cleaving sweetness,
remember you are naked here,
remember you always seek
a chorus of flesh,
there is never too much,

yet—and on the outer level—
you are moaning, "oh God, oh God,"
you are in fact
in the sort of stumbling Zen he brought,
you hear the underwater world,
it is the second, Dvorak's New World, second,
stealing air, water, legs, cloth,
air, water, satin,
possibility
that you could ever
leave.

Yet stories seek truer endings.
At first it seemed to me I would lose you
to the Caribbean, and for a single reason.
He wasn't looking for you
(I was looking,) he never
looked straight on, it was the glint
of shells, of silver on the beach,
corner of the eye and better.
The shells embroidered on your skirt that day,
the glint. Besides, ok, I know
there is no besides,
you acted enough like
you needed.
Well,
humming those molasses songs,
peach sherry about not knowing how
to win his heart and on and fucking on,
and the Caribbean was never gentle.
He found you out of the corner
of his eye, pounced,
said later you didn't seem
married, said in and through,
in and against the crevices,
I didn't come to wreck you,
your sleep, your sweet hope
of meadow, settlement, dream,
and Margo, you hadn't planned either,
so desperate, open, undependable,
not ready for what you did,
the way flesh never replicated language,
language never echoed flesh,

a cruel half mimicry you hadn't needed,
kneaded like that in a long time, ever?
Ever? You fled running, returned.

You walked to the metro, pesero, the bus,
humming sad country translated,
words about wayward flight and goodness,
theft the cruelest loss
your face, mouth stammering, sad,
the three o'clock rain, dirty tears on your face,
but you found the pearl library,
a table, the book you were looking for filled
with precise words, a particular page
marking the dance he had left,
and you knew you had broken him,
would again and again,
but the page was gone.
You looked up, unsure, into a man's eyes watching,
he followed you home, your world of rooms and rooms,
his of flesh, nothing more,
only and only
he pushed into the front room,
an easy inside parlor
world of display and chatter,
walls of topaz,
a picture of your great aunt,
windows open but never ready
for the way he kissed and kissed,
greedy (but not like you,)
the next day he came hungrier,
found you dipping Michoacán strawberries in Náhuatl
chocolate,
coatings of bitter fury, necessary pain,
the kitchen warm, full,
the purple of berenjena, jitomate, chives,
garlands of bread, corn sticking out,
he found your hands kneading, needing,
he closed in, substituted flesh,
and you fed him, why bother to lie,
you fed him that hopeful day before he
took you down,
I thought you would stay,
took you to that basement room,

the world of ancestors,
a silken camisole, ripped, chatter of thought,
you were as Caribbean as he that day
without this time the scatter, the fear,
your relatives saw that,
the patriarch still wanting you alone,
unique, distinct, his,
but not even in that mildew,
must, scents of one-time longing,
a new voice from your blue-eyed grandmother,
full-faced, eager to disturb and promote.
She looked up, eyed the Caribbean,
Said quietly, "Well, maybe.
Try. Just try."

He came back the next day,
woke you before clothes,
pushed you toward the hall,
a surprising tangle, deep as stolen light,
he caught you unaware,
beside yourself,
as ready as chorus, tender, cruel,
he pushed and it seemed at first—
this last first—
there was no resistance, no further need,
he had stopped your incessant
drive to build room after room,
inner tunnels, underground alleys,
your odd need for cul-de-sacs
embracing, confining every emerald hope,
sapphire, except . . . .

He woke you naked and early
before you sang your made-up prayer song,
found stranded chatter, old boards, shellac,
alleys for men so unforgettable,
he lifted you, your body a graceful drape,
found the thinnest room,
the long hall,
its stretch keen as his limbs,
what they could do, did,
you built that hall for him,
you can admit it now,

there were no rooms, outer, and especially
mental you did not create, all for him.
You were desperate for him,
he hadn't been looking,
you had,
he had learned your alphabet of yearning,
what your body, your inner body did,
and there he was,
a stretch of world and thought,
something you hadn't expected,
prepared for, counted on,
his dark eyes,
but then suddenly in that curving hall,
the wall a forever mahogany,
nobody around, anybody could be around,
a hall of risk, anybody could enter,
your loins, legs so slender, able, sure,
but tense until he broke through without thought,
your fears scattered
just tossed aside,
you couldn't take your hands off,
your mouth, all the pent-up past,
a dance so opportune,
the most Caribbean of all,
until you took him out of doors,
the field dense with green,
a light hovering, ready to encase,
he plied you with carnal liquor,
swept away memory and ghost,
anything could happen here,
a dance beyond notion,
beyond color, pale or dark,
a flesh hungry for more pain,
this in fact more wordless than sex,
quieter than suffering,
beyond touch and taste,
beyond shape and form,
beyond the beyond,
beyond (it must be said,)
your love for him, its volume
its helpless pity,
contraption of need,

a love beyond and beside yourself,
you left.

Sometimes, always, story is like us—
drunk. Just drunk out of mind,
looking for proper consolation.
Your story was his wealth of,
the way he ripped,
into your night clothes, his collection
of knives, his bedroom knives,
he wanted a tough victory,
but it wouldn't come.
You stayed, ran, stayed,
did things you don't like
to remember, remember.

THE TEBOT BACH MISSION

The mission of Tebot Bach is to strengthen community, to promote literacy, to broaden the audience for poetry by community outreach programs and publishing, and to demonstrate the power of poetry to transform life experiences through readings, workshops, and publications.

THE TEBOT BACH PROGRAMS

1. A poetry reading and writing workshop series for venues which serve marginalized populations such as homeless shelters, battered women's and men's shelters, nursing homes, senior citizen daycare centers, Veterans organizations, hospitals, AIDS hospices, and correctional facilities, and for schools K-College. Participating poets include: John Balaban, M.L. Liebler, Patricia Smith, Dorianne Laux, Laurence Lieberman, Richard Jones, Arthur Sze, and Carol Moldaw.

2. A poetry reading and writing workshop series for the community Southern California at large. The workshops feature local, national, and international teaching poets. Participating poets include: David St. John, Charles Webb, Wanda Coleman, Amy Gerstler, Patricia Smith, Holly Prado, Dorothy Barresi, W.D. Ehrhart, Tom Lux, Rebecca Seiferle, Suzanne Lummis, Michael Datcher, B.H. Fairchild, Cecilia Woloch, Chris Abani, and Laurel Ann Bogen, Sam Hamill, David Lehman.

3. A publishing component in order to give local and national poets a venue for publishing and distribution.

Grateful acknowledgement is given to our supporters who make our programs possible and to Golden West College in Huntington Beach, California

TEBOT BACH

HUNTINGTON BEACH • CALIFORNIA

WWW.TEBOTBACH.ORG